DAD JOKES FOR KIDS!

350+ SILLY, LAUGH-OUT-LOUD JOKES FOR THE WHOLE FAMILY!

JIMMY NIRO

sourcebooks
wonderland

Published by Sourcebooks Wonderland, and imprint of Sourcebooks Kids.
P.O. Box 4410, Naperville, Illinois 60567-4410
(630) 961-3900
sourcebookskids.com

Source of Production: Versa Press, East Peoria, Illinois, USA
Date of Production: January 2023
Run Number: 5030528

Printed and bound in the United States of America.
VP 10 9 8

TABLE OF CONTENTS

ODDBALLS & THINGS

Did you hear about the **pirate** who got his ears pierced? They say he paid about a **buck an ear**.

"Don't you hate oyings?"

"What's **an oying**?"

"This joke!"

Q: What time is it when the clock strikes thirteen?
A: Time to buy a new clock.

* * * * * * * * * * * ✳ * * * * * * * * * *

A **sheep**, a **drum**, and a **snake** fell off a cliff.
Baa-drum-hiss!

* * * * * * * * * * * ✳ * * * * * * * * * *

"Your mom told me you have
a tuba in your bathroom."

"I don't have a tuba!"

"Really? Not even a
tuba toothpaste?"

* * * * * * * * * * * ✳ * * * * * * * * * *

Q: Why can't you borrow money from a
leprechaun?
A: Because they're always a little **short**.

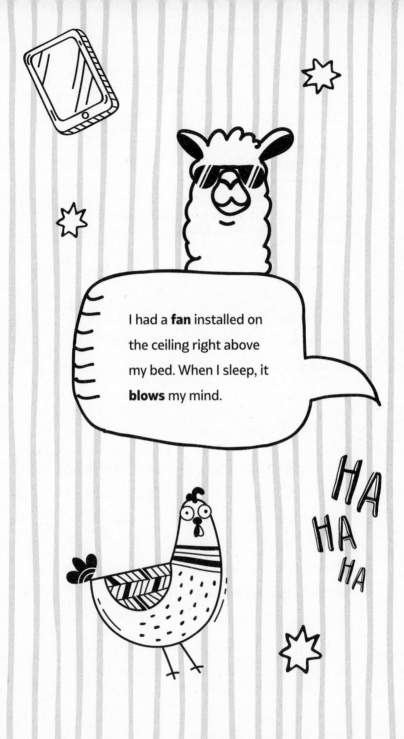

"Son, what are you doing under there?"

"Under where?"

"Ha, I made you say 'underwear!'"

Q: How did **Vikings** communicate with one another?
A: Norse code.

Two wrongs don't make a right, but three lefts do.

Q: What did one **toilet** say to the other?
A: "You look a bit **flushed**."

Once there was a **wall** who missed his best friend, who was also a wall.

He picked up the phone and called his pal.

When the wall's friend answered, the wall said, "It's been too long! We need to get together."

"I agree!" the other wall said. "Tell you what: I'll **meet you in the corner**."

* * * * * * * * * * ✭ * * * * * * * * * * *

Q: What do you call two guys **hanging on a window**?
A: **Kurt and Rod**.

* * * * * * * * * * ✭ * * * * * * * * * * *

Elevators must feel sick all the time. They're always **coming down** with something.

* * * * * * * * * * ✭ * * * * * * * * * * *

Q: What starts and ends with "E" but only has one **letter**?
A: An **envelope**.

"Why did you take your **crayons** to bed with you?"

"You told me to **draw** the curtains."

Q: What has two **legs** but can't walk?
A: A pair of **pants**.

A furniture company released a new line of **corduroy** pillows. They're making lots of head**lines**.

"Dad, why do they call the Middle Ages the **Dark** Ages?"

"There were a lot of k**nights**."

Q: Why do we dress infants in onesies?

A: Because they can't dress themselves yet!

· · · · · · · · · · · · ✶ · · · · · · · · · · ·

I had a friend once who had a bad habit of taking people's **watches**. He stole **all the time**.

· · · · · · · · · · · · ✶ · · · · · · · · · · ·

"Dad, why do people **paint eggs at Easter?**"

"I guess it's easier than **wallpapering** them."

· · · · · · · · · · · · ✶ · · · · · · · · · · ·

My friend invented a gadget that steals people's ideas and then **wipes their memory**. Why didn't I think of that?

Did you hear about the **martial artist** who had to stay home from school? He had the **kung-flu**.

· · · · · · · · · · · ✖ · · · · · · · · · · · · · ·

My mom lost her car keys this morning. She proceeded to look everywhere for them. She checked behind the cushions on the couch. She looked under the bed. She dug through her desk drawers.

Finally, she found them in the pocket of her winter coat. "Ugh!" she said with frustration. "Why are my keys always in the last place I look?"

I wasn't sure if she wanted an answer, but I had one anyway.

"Because when you find something, you stop looking for it!"

· · · · · · · · · · · ✖ · · · · · · · · · · · · · ·

Q: How do you make a **tissue** dance?
A: Put a little **boogie** in it.

Q: Which **rock group** features four former presidents?

A: **Mount Rushmore**.

· · · · · · · · · · ✦ · · · · · · · · · ·

"Happy Father's Day, Dad!"

"Thanks, **Son**! But remember: it's also **Son**day."

· · · · · · · · · · ✦ · · · · · · · · · ·

I spent five minutes fixing a broken clock this morning. At least, I think it was five minutes.

· · · · · · · · · · ✦ · · · · · · · · · ·

Q: What's blue and doesn't **weigh** very much?

A: **Light** blue.

I don't know why anyone would fill a box with **two thousand pieces of cardboard**. Seriously, I'm **puzzle**d.

· · · · · · · · · · ✸ · · · · · · · · · ·

Q: What did the **digital** clock say to the grandfather clock?
A: "Look! **No hands!**"

· · · · · · · · · · ✸ · · · · · · · · · ·

"I can't **stand** your jokes, Dad!"

"Have you tried **sitting** down?"

· · · · · · · · · · ✸ · · · · · · · · · ·

Balloon animals are fun, but they aren't very smart. In fact, I'd go so far as to call them **air**heads.

Q: Why do people wear **sham**rocks on St. Patrick's Day?

A: Regular rocks are too heavy.

* * *

The hardware store is selling ten bags of **soil** for only fifteen dollars. That's **dirt** cheap!

* * *

My grandmother gave me the best advice I'd ever heard the other day. She said, "Remember these two words. They'll **open** a lot of doors for you in life: **push and pull**."

* * *

My dad thinks my **runny nose** is funny, but it's **snot**!

* * *

Q: When is your mind like a rumpled **bed**?

A: When it isn't **made up** yet.

When I saw my uncle for the first time in a while, he said to me, "Wow! You must have grown **a foot** since I saw you last!"

I replied, "No. I still have **two**."

. . . . ✳ . . . .

I love going out**doors**. It's much safer than going out**windows**.

. . . . ✳ . . . .

Q: What do you call a **denim** expert?
A: A **jean**ius.

"What's the difference between a piano, a tuna, and a tube of glue?"

"I don't know. What?"

"You can tune a piano, but you can't piano a tuna!"

"But what about the **glue**?"

"I knew you'd get **stuck** there."

* * * ✳ * * * *

I found a **four-leaf clover**. It looked a little crumpled but was otherwise intact. My friend told me I should iron it to make it look a bit better, but I declined. I didn't want to press my **luck**.

"Dad, how tall is the Empire State Building?"

"I'd say it's about one Empire State Building tall."

My dad asked to borrow my **large** grandfather **clock**. He owes me **big time**.

I was working on a crossword puzzle, but couldn't quite put my finger on the word for one of the last clues.

"Can I help?" my friend asked.

"Sure," I said. "The clue is '**mailman**'s bag.'"

"How many **letters**?" she asked.

"Oh," I replied. "Loads of them!"

A+ FUNNIES

"Why are you **eating** your homework?"

"My teacher said it would be a **piece of cake**!"

Q: Why did the girl cross to the other side of the **playground**?

A: To get to the other **slide**.

HA HA HA

Once upon a time, there was a little girl who showed up to school carrying a **ladder**. When she got to class, she set up the ladder and climbed it up to the top. Her teachers were confused and asked her what she was doing.

She answered simply, "I wanted to go to **high** school."

• • • • • • • • • ⭐ • • • • • • • • •

Q: What do you call the **king** of all school supplies?
A: The **ruler**.

• • • • • • • • • ⭐ • • • • • • • • •

"Dad, what happens to **pencils** when we stop using them?"

"They go on vacation."

"To where?"

"**Pencil**vania."

The most popular kid in my high school was a **calendar**. Let me tell you: he had so many **dates**!

· · · · · · · · · · · ✳ · · · · · · · · · · · ·

"Time to get up for school, kids!"

"Dad, can I have a few more minutes? I'm trying to **catch** up on sleep."

LOL

"Have you tried **chasing it** around your bed?"

· · · · · · · · · · · ✳ · · · · · · · · · · · ·

Q: Why was the **broom** late for school?
A: It over**swept**.

· · · · · · · · · · · ✳ · · · · · · · · · · · ·

School must have been easier for cavemen. They didn't have much history to study.

Q: What is a **bubble**'s favorite thing to do at school?
A: Take **pop** quizzes!

HA HA HA

"Dad, which building has the most **stories**?"

"I'd have to guess the **library**."

<hr />

Q: Why is "dark" spelled with a K and not a C?
A: Because you can't **C in the dark**.

<hr />

When I was in school, my teacher liked to tease us. One day, we came into class and she told us she had an announcement to make.

"Class, we have decided to have a half day of school this morning," she said, and all of the students cheered.

Then she continued, "We will then have the other half of the day this afternoon."

Q: Where did the **ice cream** truck driver go to school?

A: Sundae school.

* * *

Q: Why did the **nose** want to stay home from school?

A: He was tired of getting **picked** on.

* * *

"Dad, what should I do if my teacher **rolls** her eyes at me?"

"**Roll** them back to her!"

* * *

Q: What did the **pencil sharpener** say to the pencil?

A: "Stop **going in circles** and get to the point."

"When I was in school, my teacher wore **sunglasses** to class all the time."

"Why did she do that?"

"We were all really **bright**."

* * * * * * * ✳ * * * * * * *

Q: Why do the students in the **geometry** class always get tired halfway through?
A: They're out of **shape**.

* * * * * * * ✳ * * * * * * *

When I was in school, I didn't see the purpose of learning **decimals**. But now, I have to say, there is a **point**.

* * * * * * * ✳ * * * * * * *

Q: Why is the playground larger during **recess**?
A: There are more **feet** in it.

The science teacher was explaining an extremely important concept to his students.

"This lesson is going to come up on the test," he said. "I'm going to try to make it as **clear** as I can, but pay attention."

Then he wrote the lesson down on the **window**.

"Dad, you told me that there were **twenty-five** letters in the alphabet, but my teacher says there are twenty-six. Why did you tell me that?"

"I don't know **Y**."

Q: Why were the fish's parents upset about his **grades**?

A: They were below **C**-level.

"Dad, I think my school is **haunted**."

"Why do you say that?"

"My teachers keep talking about school **spirit**."

Q: What is a **snake**'s favorite subject in school?
A: **Hiss**tory.

Q: What happens once every **m**inute but never in a decade?
A: The letter "**M**."

Did you hear about the **letters** that didn't make it into the alphabet? They got lost in the **mail**.

"My dad felt **stung** when I showed him my report card."

"How come? Were your grades that bad?"

"Not too bad! I got mostly A's, but there were also a couple **bees** on there."

· · · · · · · · · · · · · · · · · · · · · · · · · ·

"Dad, are you smart?"

"Yes, I believe I am."

"Can you spell it?"

"Sure. S-M-A-R-T."

"You said you're smart, but you can't even spell the word 'it.'"

Q: What do you call a teacher who doesn't **fart** in public?

A: A private **toot**or.

- - - - - - - ✦ - - - - - - -

Q: What word has five letters but becomes shorter when you add two more?

A: **Short**.

- - - - - - - ✦ - - - - - - -

"Dad, I just saw a whole **school** of fish!"

"You should try to catch them!"

"How?"

"**Book**worms."

JOKING JOCKS

Q: What do you call a pig that knows **karate**?
A: A pork **chop**.

Q: What kind of animals spend all their time at **baseball** games?
A: **Bats**!

Porcupines win every game. They always have the most **points**.

Q: Why aren't **pastries** very good at basketball?

A: Too many **turnovers**!

. . . . ✳ . . . .

Q: Why did the baseball player only spend **five minutes** at the store?

A: It was a **short stop**.

. . . . ✳ . . . .

Q: What can you **catch** but not throw?

A: A **cold**.

. . . . ✳ . . . .

Magicians are great at hockey. They always have **hat tricks**.

. . . . ✳ . . . .

Q: What has eighteen legs and catches **flies**?

A: A **baseball** team.

During halftime, the football coach went to the breakroom across from the locker room and tried to buy a drink from the vending machine. Unfortunately, the vending machine ate his **money**.

"I want my **quarter** back!" he yelled at the machine.

A moment later, the quarterback, Tom, stuck his head out of the locker room.

"What do you need, coach?" he asked.

Q: Why did the **basketball** player bring a suitcase to the game?

A: The referee kept telling him he **traveled** a lot.

Q: What do you call a girl standing in the **middle of a tennis court**?

A: Annette.

Q: What do you call a wizard who loves to play **golf**?

A: Harry **Putter**.

· · · · · · · · · ⭐ · · · · · · · · · ·

I'm not a fan of **bowling**. It's just not up my **alley**.

· · · · · · · · · ⭐ · · · · · · · · · ·

Q: Why didn't the **rope** win the race?

A: It was **tied**.

· · · · · · · · · ⭐ · · · · · · · · · ·

Q: Why did the **police officers** go to the baseball game?

A: They'd gotten reports of someone **stealing** a base.

· · · · · · · · · ⭐ · · · · · · · · · ·

Q: What's a **baseball** player's least favorite Star Wars movie?

A: *The* **Umpire** *Strikes Back.*

I was out **fishing** with my best friend. We talked for a while, but after a bit, we decided we should listen to some music while we fished.

"What do you want to hear?" she asked me, looking through her phone for the perfect song.

I said, "Probably something **catchy**."

Q: What do Olympic **sprinters** eat before their races?

A: Nothing. They **fast**.

Q: What do a **baseball** team and a **pancake** have in common?

A: They both need a good **batter**.

The Yankees recently recruited a **snail** to play for them. Some people were surprised, but I hear he's a real **slug**ger.

Q: Why did the **cabbage** win the race?
A: It was **a head**.

* * * * * ✦ * * * * *

Q: What sport can you play on a **carpet**?
A: **Rug**by.

* * * * * ✦ * * * * *

When I was in high school and on the **track** team, my coach would tell the same joke repeatedly throughout the season. It was a **running** gag.

* * * * * ✦ * * * * *

Q: Why did the pro **football** player eat soup every day?
A: He wanted to take part in a **Souper Bowl**!

* * * * * ✦ * * * * *

Q: Which baseball player should you ask for a **glass of water**?
A: The **pitcher**.

ON-THE-GO GAGS

Q: What's the **cheapest** way to travel?
A: In a **sale** boat.

My dog chases everyone on a bicycle. I'm finally going to have to take his bike away.

Q: What's a **car**'s favorite meal?
A: **Brake**fast.

Have you ever traveled on a flying **carpet**? It is such a **rug**ged experience.

Q: How does a race car **clean** the house?
A: With a **broom broom**!

What do we want?! **Race car** noises! When do we want them?! **Neeeeeeoooooooowwwwww**!

Q: What kind of lights did **Noah** have on the Ark?
A: **Flood**lights.

Q: What do you call a **boat** with a hole at the bottom?
A: A **sink**.

"Dad, how does the Easter **Bunny** get around the world?"

"He flies, just like Santa."

"You mean in a sleigh with reindeer?"

"No, in a **hare** plane!"

Q: What do you call a **boat** with a hole at the bottom?
A: A **sink**.

My car horn wasn't working, so I took it to a friend of mine who was a **Boy Scout**. He worked on it for a few minutes and then told me: "**Beep repaired**."

Q: What do you call a **bus** that can cross the ocean?

A: Christopher Colum**bus**.

· · · · · · · · · · · · · · · · · · · · · · · · ·

"Dad, can you help me with my geography homework?"

"Sure. What's the question?"

"Where are the Great **Plains** located?"

"Oh, that's an easy one. At the **airport**."

· · · · · · · · · · · · · · · · · · · · · · · ·

Q: What's the difference between a teacher and a train?

A: The teacher tells you to spit your gum out; the **train** says, "**chew, chew, chew**."

Did you hear about the new **monorail**? It's **engine**-eous.

. . . . ✶ . . . .

Q: What kind of car does **Mickey Mouse**'s wife drive?
A: A **Minnie** van.

. . . . ✶ . . . .

When the **wheel** was invented, it really started a **revolution**.

. . . . ✶ . . . .

Q: What kind of vehicle has four wheels and **flies**?
A: A **garbage** truck!

. . . . ✶ . . . .

Q: What happened to the **frog** that parked illegally?
A: He got **toad**.

PLANT-ASTIC
NATURE PUNS

Q: What kind of tree fits into your **hand**?
A: A **palm** tree.

· · · · · · · · · · · · · · · · · · ·

Q: What washes up on tiny **beaches**?
A: Micro**waves**.

· · · · · · · · · · · · · · · · · · ·

I've always been afraid of **rock** climbing. I'd try it if
I were **boulder**.

"Dad, what is a **full** moon?"

"When it's had **enough to eat**, I guess."

- - - - - - - ✶ - - - - - - -

Q: What do you get when you toss a pile of **books** into the ocean?
A: A **title** wave.

LOL

- - - - - - - ✶ - - - - - - -

It's been **foggy** for days, but it looks like the weather is clearing up. The fog won't be **mist**.

- - - - - - - ✶ - - - - - - -

Q: Why are forests so **noisy**?
A: The trees all have **bark**.

Q: What candy can you find in a swamp?
A: Marshmallows.

My most magical Christmas was when it started **snowing** right as the clock struck midnight on Christmas Eve. It was **white** on time.

Q: Where do **lamps** like to sit at the beach?
A: In the **shade**.

Once there was a little **flower** planted next to an oak tree. It was struggling to grow. No matter how much the people in the nearby house watered the flower, it just wouldn't flourish.

One day, the flower was on the verge of giving up. "I'll never grow tall and blossom into a beautiful flower," she said. "It's hopeless!"

The **oak tree** responded with encouragement, "I'm **root**ing for you!"

I always know I'll have a good time when we go to the **beach**. It's a **shore** thing.

* * *

A **lawn** is more dangerous than most people think. It's full of **blades**!

* * *

Q: If April showers bring May flowers, what do **May flowers** bring?
A: Pilgrims!

* * *

I know why no aliens have come to Earth yet. They checked the **reviews** for our solar system and only saw **one star**!

* * *

Q: What do you call a **fake** stone?
A: A **sham**rock.

Q: How do you make a waterbed more **bouncy**?

A: Add **spring** water.

. . . . ✶ . . . .

I was on a walk through the woods with my kids.

"I think someone must have been **cutting wood** back there," I told them, pointing at a clearing we'd passed through about fifty yards back.

"How do you know?" my daughter asked.

"I **sawdust**."

. . . . ✶ . . . .

Q: Why did the minnow cross the **ocean**?

A: To get to the other **tide**.

. . . . ✶ . . . .

Q: Where do naughty **rainbows** go?

A: **Prism**.

HA HA
HA

I'm fascinated by **water in the air**. It **mist**ifies me.

⁎

Q: What did one **fern** say to another?
A: "We'll be best **fronds** forever."

⁎

Q: What's the richest kind of **air**?
A: Million**aire**.

⁎

Two long-lost **fish** friends ran into each other in the ocean one day.

"Hey," said the first fish. "I haven't seen you in a while!"

"Yeah!" said the other. "Long time, no **sea**!"

⁎

Q: What do **trees** eat in the morning?
A: **Oak**meal.

OTTERLY GOOFY ANIMALS

Q: What do you call a b**ear** with no ears?
A: B.

Q: Which bird is in need of a **wig**?
A: A **bald** eagle.

My dog **cries** all the time, but I think it's because of his breed. He's a Chi-**wah-wah**.

Q: What do you get when you cross an **elephant** with a fish?

A: Swimming **trunks**.

Q: What did the **Dalmatian** say when she finished her lunch?

A: "That hit the **spot**."

Q: What kind of haircut does a **bee** get?

A: A **buzz** cut.

Q: What kind of bird are you most likely to find on a **construction** site?

A: A **crane**.

Once, there was a **cow** who produced no milk. No matter how hard she tried, she just couldn't make any milk appear.

"It's hopeless," she told her best friend one day. "I'm an **udder** failure."

· · · · · · · · · ✳ · · · · · · · · · ·

Q: What do you call an elephant in a phone booth?

A: Stuck!

· · · · · · · · · ✳ · · · · · · · · · ·

Once there was a **porcupine** who didn't know who his parents were.

"How do I find my parents?" he asked his friend, the aardvark, one day.

"Just look for someone who looks similar to you and ask if they're your mom or dad," the aardvark said wisely.

So the porcupine searched and searched until he found someone who looked a bit like him.

"Are you my mommy?" he asked the **cactus**.

Q: What do you call a **sleeping** bull?

A: A bull**dozer**.

Q: What's the **sneakiest** fish in the sea?

A: The **shhhh**ark.

Q: What was the first **animal** in space?

A: The **cow** that jumped over the moon!

A dad went to the pet store because his kids had convinced him to buy them a kitten. He was willing to get a cat, but he didn't want to spend too much money.

"Do you have any kittens going **cheap**?" the dad asked the store owner.

"Oh, no, sir," the owner said, looking confused. "All our kittens go *meow*."

Q: What's a **penguin**'s favorite aunt?

A: Aunt **Arctica**.

· · · · · · · · ✦ · · · · · · · · ·

"My teacher told us that farmer ants were the **smartest** type of insect."

"Really? I don't think that's right."

"What insect do you think is smarter?"

"A **spelling** bee!"

· · · · · · · · ✦ · · · · · · · · ·

Q: Where do **otters** come from?

A: **Otter** space.

Birds really live fast lives. Time just **flies** by.

. . . . ✳ . . . .

Q: What did one **firefly** say to encourage the other?
A: "You **glow**, girl!"

. . . . ✳ . . . .

Q: What does a **turtle** do on its birthday?
A: It **shell**ebrates!

. . . . ✳ . . . .

It was tense at the mission control center when they launched a **cow** into space. They said it was a high-**steaks** mission.

Q: What's the difference between a cat and a complex sentence?

A: A cat has **claws** at the end of its **paws**; a complex sentence has a **pause** at the end of its **clause**!

. . . . ✳ . . . .

"Dad, why do cows wear cow**bells**?"

"Their **horns** must not work."

. . . . ✳ . . . .

Q: What's the difference between a **silly** rabbit and an **athletic** rabbit?

A: One's a bit **funny** and the other's a **fit** bunny!

. . . . ✳ . . . .

Q: What did the **worm** say to his daughter when she came home late?

A: "Where on **Earth** have you been?"

Jayden the **giraffe** was struggling in school. He was having so much trouble keeping up with the rest of the animals in his class that his teacher even called his parents in for a special meeting.

"What seems to be the problem?" Jayden's mom asked. "Is Jayden being disruptive during class?"

"Actually, he's been daydreaming," the teacher said. "His **head is always in the clouds**!"

Q: How did the **beaver** get on Facebook?
A: He **log**ged on.

There are two **birds** at our bird feeder that seem to be in love. You could say they're each other's **tweet**hearts.

Q: What's the most **famous** fish?
A: The **star**fish!

. . . . ✳ . . . .

I once met a **llama** who had a lot of far-fetched end-of-the-world theories. He really believed in the **alpaca**lypse.

. . . . ✳ . . . .

Q: What do you call a **bee** that can't make up its mind?
A: A may**bee**.

. . . . ✳ . . . .

Q: What happens when you cross a **sheep** with a **cow**?
A: You get an animal in a **baa**aaaaaaad **moo**oooooood.

"Dad, I keep trying to get these **ants** to go away, but they won't!"

"I guess you could call them perman**ant**."

* * * * * * * * * * * * ✳ * * * * * * * * * * * *

Q: What is a **hyena**'s favorite type of candy?
A: Snickers.

TASTY
TRICKS

"Dad, can I have some **short**bread?"

"Afraid not!"

"How come?"

"They aren't making it any **long**er."

Q: What has **ears** but can't hear?
A: A **cornfield**.

Q: What do you call cheese when it's all **by itself**?
A: Prov**alone**.

· · · · · · · · · · · · · · · · · · · · · · · ·

"Son, what do you call the lunch meat that tastes like hot dogs?"

"**Bologna**."

"This isn't bologna. It's a serious question!"

· · · · · · · · · · · · · · · · · · · · · · · ·

Kittens on Mars must have trouble drinking **milk**. It's all in flying **saucers**!

One time when your mom wasn't home, I got hungry and ordered a pizza. The delivery driver arrived and was rude to me, so I asked him the only question I could think of.

"Hey, you wanna **pizza** me?!"

Every time the **bee** tried to comb her hair, it ended up sticky.

"Why does this keep happening?" she asked her friends. "I just want my hair to be smooth and straight!"

"I can see what the problem is," one of her friends said. "You keep using a **honey comb**."

Q: How do you make a **milk**shake?
A: Put a **cow** on a roller coaster.

I got fired from my job at the **orange juice** factory. They told me it was because of my lack of **concentration**.

Q: What starts with a T, ends with a T, and is full of T?
A: A teapot.

Q: Why couldn't the **butter** leave the casino?
A: Because it was **on a roll**!

"Dad, how do you make an egg **roll**?"

"It's easy. You just **push it**."

I know a few a**maize**ing jokes about **corn**.

Q: When potatoes have **kids**, what are they called?
A: Tater **tots**.

Q: What is yellow and something you shouldn't drink?
A: A school bus.

Q: What is a **toad**'s favorite type of soda?
A: **Croak**-a-Cola

One night, my dad was preparing dinner. He'd been plan-ning to cut up a cantaloupe so that the family could have fruit with the meal. For some reason, though, he couldn't find it in the kitchen.

"Oliver," he called to me. "Have you seen the melon that was on the counter?"

I walked in looking guilty. "Yes, Dad," I said.

"Where is it?" he asked.

"It's in the **bathtub**," I responded.

Dad was confused and a little angry. "Why would you put the melon in the bathtub?" he asked.

I replied, "I wanted it to be **water**melon."

Q: Where do hamburgers go to **dance**?
A: The meat**ball**!

Q: What do you get when you cross a **monkey** with a peach?
A: An **ape**ricot!

A family was eating dinner. At the end of the meal, the youngest daughter asked to be excused.

"Not until you've eaten your carrots," her dad said.

"But I hate carrots!" she said. "They taste yucky."

"Even so," said the dad. "It's important to eat your carrots because carrots are good for your eyes."

"How do you know?" the girl asked.

"Well," said the dad. "You've never seen a bunny wearing glasses, have you?"

* * * ✦ * * *

Q: What's a **scarecrow**'s favorite fruit?
A: **Straw**berries.

* * * ✦ * * *

"Dad, what are you making for breakfast? It smells good."

"**Pancakes**. They are going to be **flipping** good."

Q: What's worse than finding a worm in your apple?

A: Finding half a worm in your apple.

Q: What did the **salt** say to the **pepper**?

A: "What's **shakin**'?"

I don't like **sour**dough bread. It always has the worst **attitude**.

Q: How did the jury find the **hamburger**?

A: **Grill**ty as charred!

"Dad, why do fish swim in salt water?"

"Because **pepper** water would make them **sneeze!**"

Q: What did the carrot say to the broccoli?
A: Nothing. Vegetables can't talk.

I thought about going on an all-**almond** diet, but that's just **nuts**.

Q: Is it proper to eat with your **fingers**?
A: No, you should eat with your **mouth**!

Q: What did the confrontational **cake** say?
A: "You want a **piece** of me?!"

I was shopping in a grocery store once when one of the produce employees asked if I wanted to hear a riddle.

"Sure," I told her.

"When you drive, you go on green and stop on red," she said. "When do you go on red and stop on green?"

I thought for a minute, but I couldn't come up with the right answer. I asked, "When?"

She smiled at me and said, "When you're eating a watermelon!"

Q: What does **bread** wear to bed?
A: **Jam**mies.

I heard a bad joke about **food**. It was hard to **digest**.

· · · · · · · · · · · · ✳ · · · · · · · · · · · · ·

A family of **rabbits** was sitting down to dinner. Once everyone was seated and all the plates were on the table, the oldest rabbit nodded when it was time to begin.

"Okay," she said. "**Lettuce** eat."

DINOS, MONSTERS & GHOSTS, OH MY!

I thought there was a real **dinosaur** in the house,
but it was just a **fossil**-arm.

. . . .

Q: How can you tell if a **vampire** has a cold?
A: See if he starts **coffin**.

. . . . ✶ . . . .

Q: What do you call a ghost's **mom** and **dad**?
A: Trans**parents**.

"Dad, how much does a **dragon** weigh?"

"It depends on the **scales**."

* * *

Q: What do you call a dinosaur playing **hide and seek**?
A: A do-you-think-he-**saw**-us.

* * *

It took the abominable snowman four hours to **finish** a book. He just wasn't that **hungry**.

* * *

Q: What time is it when Godzilla comes to school?
A: Time to run!

Ghosts never have money problems. They don't have to worry about the cost of **living**.

Q: Which dinosaur had the best **vocabulary**?
A: The **thesaurus**.

Q: Why couldn't the monster fall asleep?
A: It was afraid kids were under the bed.

"Dad, come look! I found a giant **snail**!"

"Was it on the end of a giant's **finger**?"

I heard **Dracula** didn't have a lot of friends in school. They all said he was a pain in the **neck**.

· · · · · · · · · ✳ · · · · · · · ·

Q: Who was Albert Einstein's **evil** twin?
A: Frank**einstein**.

· · · · · · · · · ✳ · · · · · · · ·

Q: Why didn't the dragon eat the **clown**?
A: He thought it would taste **funny**.

· · · · · · · · · ✳ · · · · · · · ·

Did you hear about the **ghost** that went to the drugstore to buy a box of bandages? He had a lot of **boo-boos**!

· · · · · · · · · ✳ · · · · · · · ·

Q: Why didn't anyone want to kiss **Dracula**?
A: They say he had **bat** breath.

Q: What do **spirits** send to their friends when they go on vacation?

A: Ghostcards!

. . . . ✦ . . . .

Have you heard about the **mythical creature** who always hogs the spotlight? He just has to be the **centaur** of attention.

. . . . ✦ . . . .

Q: How did the vampire **sail** across the ocean?

A: In a blood **vessel**.

. . . . ✦ . . . .

The two-headed monster was always at the top of his class. I guess **two heads** are better than one.

. . . . ✦ . . . .

Q: What do you call a werewolf on a spaceship?

A: An **elsewhere**wolf.

Q: How do monsters like their **eggs**?
A: Terri**fried**.

* * *

Did you hear about the monster with **eight arms**?
He says they come in **handy**.

* * *

Q: How do you ask a dinosaur out on a **date**?
A: "**Tea**, Rex?"

* * *

Q: Why don't **ghosts** like rain on Halloween?
A: It dampens their **spirits**.

SILLY STEM

I know a **robot** who isn't afraid of anything. He has nerves of **steel**.

Q: What's an **astronaut**'s favorite part of a computer?
A: The **space**bar.

I wonder how Benjamin Franklin felt when he discovered **electricity**. I bet he was **shocked**!

Q: Which weighs more: a ton of feathers or a ton of bricks?
A: They both weigh a ton.

. . . . ✳ . . . .

"Son, take your age and add five years to it."

"Okay. Then what? Is this a math quiz?"

"That's your age in five years!"

. . . . ✳ . . . .

I feel bad for batteries. They always **die** but never **live**.

. . . . ✳ . . . .

Q: What does a computer do when it's **tired**?
A: It **crashes**.

Q: Why did the student get upset when her teacher called her **average**?

A: It was a **mean** thing to say!

I asked my son if he could hand me the newspaper. He told me that newspapers were old-school and that he liked to read his tablet instead.

"Here," he said, handing me his iPad. "You can get way more out of this than any newspaper."

That fly didn't stand a chance.

Q: Where do students in New York City learn **multiplication**?

A: **Times** Square.

Q: Why was the **computer** cold?

A: It left the **Windows** open.

"Dad, you know what's really **odd**?"

"Numbers not divisible by two?"

- - - - - - - - - - ✶ - - - - - - - - - - -

Q: What do you call a bee that comes from **America**?

A: USB.

- - - - - - - - - - ✶ - - - - - - - - - - -

"Dad, I think our computer has a **virus**. What should we do?"

"Take it to the **doctor**!"

- - - - - - - - - - ✶ - - - - - - - - - - -

My grandfather's last words were, "**Gallons. Quarts. Liters.**" That spoke **volumes**.

"Dad, is **time travel** real?"

"Oh yeah. I actually have a time machine."

"Really? Why haven't I seen it?"

"I only use it from **time to time**."

There was a **fight** between nineteen and twenty. Twenty **one**.

Q: Do you know why there's the saying "Be there or be **square**"?
A: Because you're not a**round**.

I was looking for photos of **spiders**. I found them on the **web**.

Q: What is a **mathematician**'s favorite dessert?

A: Pumpkin **Pi**.

BOREDOM BUSTERS

When flying through space, Luke Skywalker and his droid decided to take the **long way around** an asteroid field. It was an R2-**Detour**.

* * * * * * * * * ★ * * * * * * * * *

Q: What does **Pac-Man** eat with his chips?
A: Guaca**waka**mole.

Bert and Ernie were out at the park when they heard an ice cream truck.

Bert asked Ernie, "Would you like some ice cream?"

Ernie replied, "Sher**bert**."

A **book** just fell on my head! It really hurt, but I've only got my **shelf** to blame.

Q: Why did **Goofy** go to outer space?

A: To find **Pluto**.

Q: What did Snow White say when her **photos** weren't ready?

A: "Someday, my **prints** will come."

"Dad, do you play any instruments?"

"I used to play the **trombone**, but I let it **slide**."

***

Books must be scared all the time. They're always hiding under their **covers**.

***

"Dad, why is the iPod in the **refrigerator**?"

"You kids said I needed to listen to **cooler** music."

***

If Batman were a **tree**, we would call him **Spruce** Wayne.

Q: What do you call a rabbit with **fleas**?
A: Bugs Bunny!

. . . . ✶ . . . .

I put your **grandma** on speed dial. Now she's an Insta**gran**.

. . . . ✶ . . . .

Q: How do **cows** entertain themselves?
A: They go to the **moo**vies.

. . . . ✶ . . . .

"Dad, I heard this song called 'Colors of the Wind' and it made me wonder—what color is the **wind**?"

"**Blew**."

Q: What's the loudest kind of **pet**?
A: A trum**pet**!

· · · · · · · · · ✳ · · · · · · · · · ·

I almost got caught stealing a **board game**, but it was a **Risk** I was willing to take.

· · · · · · · · · ✳ · · · · · · · · · ·

"Dad, we're reading **Harry Potter** in school."

"Oh really? I love Harry Potter!"

"How would you rate it on a scale of one to ten?"

"I'd say about **nine and three quarters**."

Q: What's a **bunny** rabbit's favorite type of music?
A: Hip-**hop**.

. . . . * . . . .

I went to **Lego**land as a kid. People were lined up for **blocks**.

. . . . * . . . .

Q: Why couldn't the **piano** figure out how to unlock the door to his house?
A: He had eighty-eight **keys**!

. . . . * . . . .

"Your mom and I are going to see a movie."

"What's it about?"

"I think it's about two hours."

Q: Who taught Luke Skywalker how to make **pastries**?
A: Obi-Wan **Cannoli**.

· · · · · · · · · · · ✳ · · · · · · · · · ·

You can't ever give **Elsa** a balloon. She'll just **let it go**.

· · · · · · · · · · · ✳ · · · · · · · · · ·

"Dad, can we go see this new movie about **pirates**?"

"I don't think so. You're not allowed to see that movie."

"What?! How come?"

"Because it's rated **ARRRRR**!"

"Dad, I've decided I want to play **bass**."

"Great! Just try not to get into **treble**."

* * * ✳ * * *

Q: What did Tarzan say when he saw a herd of elephants coming?
A: "Here come the elephants!"

* * * ✳ * * *

I've heard that **balloons** are really scared of music. Especially **pop** music.

* * * ✳ * * *

Q: What's a **tornado**'s favorite game to play?
A: Twister.

"Dad, do you want to play a **board** game with us?"

"I'd rather play an **entertained** game!"

Q: Why does Superman get invited to so many **dinner** parties?
A: He's a **supper**hero!

HARD-WORKING HUMOR

I'll tell you what: getting paid to **sleep** would be my **dream** job.

One time, I went to see a Spanish magician.

"For my last trick, I will make myself disappear," he told us at the end of the night. "I will count to **three** and then I will be gone."

And so he counted.

"*Uno*," he said. I leaned forward in anticipation.

"*Dos*," he said. I was really excited to see what would happen next.

Then he vanished without a *tres*.

Q: What did the **fireman** name his two sons?

A: José and **Hose**-B.

. . . . * . . . .

Did you hear about the **bakery** that hired a pig as the head chef? I guess he was really good at **bacon**.

. . . . * . . . .

The **police officer** was getting dressed for work when he noticed a mouse moving underneath his **clothing** on the dresser.

"Freeze!" he said. "You're under a **vest**!"

. . . . * . . . .

My **eye doctor** is running for president. Some people say she doesn't have a chance, but I think she's a real **vision**ary.

A **gingerbread man** hired a building team to construct him a new house. When the house was done, it was a true work of art, covered in sugar, frosting, gumdrops, and candy.

When the gingerbread saw it, he was so excited about the new house that he could only manage one word: "**Sweet!**"

Q: What do you call a dentist who fixes a crocodile's teeth?
A: Really brave.

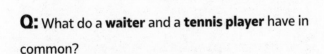

Two **artists** were arguing about who was better. The argument ended in a **draw**.

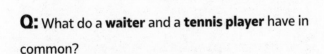

Q: What do a **waiter** and a **tennis player** have in common?
A: They're both great at **serving**.

"Kids, I have a riddle for you."

"What is it?"

"There once was a **butcher** who wore an XXL shirt, a size-fourteen shoe, and the biggest gloves he could find. What did he weigh?"

"I don't know, but it sounds like a lot."

"**Meat**."

· · · · · · · · · · ✳ · · · · · · · · · ·

All **shoemakers** must go to heaven. They have good **soles**.

· · · · · · · · · · ✳ · · · · · · · · · ·

Q: What is an **astronaut**'s favorite snack food?
A: **Rocket** chips.

"My teacher is out for the week. She's on her honeymoon."

"Oh yeah? Who did she marry?"

"The school **janitor**."

"I bet he **swept** her off her feet."

· · · · · · · · ✳ · · · · · · · · · ·

Q: What do you call a **sleepwalking** nun?
A: A **roam**in' Catholic.

· · · · · · · · ✳ · · · · · · · · · ·

I got a job as a **baker**, but had to quit. I couldn't make enough **dough**.

· · · · · · · · ✳ · · · · · · · · · ·

The neighbors hired a snake to **build** the new addition on their house. He's a boa **constructor**.

It was busy at the doctor's office. The doctor was trying to see all her patients but was running behind.

"Doctor," a nurse said. "There's an **invisible man** in the waiting room."

The doctor was flustered. "Tell him I **can't see him** right now!"

* * * ✶ * * *

Did you hear about the man who lost his job at the **coin** factory? They say he stopped making **cents**.

* * * ✶ * * *

One morning, a **farmer** came into his barn to find that his favorite cow was missing. For a moment, he worried that he might never see her again. Luckily, he **tractor** down.

* * * ✶ * * *

Q: What do dentists call their **X-ray scans**?
A: Tooth **pics**.

A member of the royal family decided to move to the country and **grow corn**. You could say he was Prince **Farming**.

* * * * * * * * * * ✳ * * * * * * * * * *

Q: Why do **astronomers** put beef in their shampoo?
A: For **meatier** showers.

* * * * * * * * * * ✳ * * * * * * * * * *

A detective asked a man to come downtown for an interview. When they arrived, the investigator asked, "Where were you from **five to six**?"

The man replied, "**Kindergarten**."

* * * * * * * * * * ✳ * * * * * * * * * *

If you have a bad **altitude**, you cannot be a good **pilot**.

DAD JOKE WORDPLAY

(Fill in the blanks to complete the jokes!)

Q: What did the _____ say to the
(noun)
bread?

A: Quit **loaf**ing around.

· · · · · · · · · · · · · · ✦ · · · · · · · · · · · ·

Q: If you drop a _____ into the **ocean**,
(noun)
what does it become?

A: Wet!

Q: What do you do if you see a **blue** _____?
(noun)

A: Try to **cheer** it up.

· · · · · · · · ✳ · · · · · · · · ·

I don't just love **condiments** on my _____, I **relish** them!
(food)

· · · · · · · · ✳ · · · · · · · · ·

Q: What do you call a man who _____ on
(verb)

your **door**step?

A: Matt.

· · · · · · · · ✳ · · · · · · · · ·

Q: What's the best dessert to enjoy while watching a **scary** _____?
(noun)

A: I **scream**!

Q: Why did the **teddy bear** say no to _____?
(food)
A: He was **stuffed**.

- - - - - - - ✕ - - - - - - -

Q: What stays in **one corner** but still _____
(verb)
all over the world?
A: A **postage stamp**!

- - - - - - - ✕ - - - - - - -

I got _____ a **fridge** for their birthday.
(person)
I can't wait to see their face **light up** when they
open it.

- - - - - - - ✕ - - - - - - -

Q: How did the **clam** get to the _____?
(place)
A: By **shell**icopter.

Q: What do **cowboys** like on their _____?
(food)
A: Ranch dressing.

· · · · · · · · ✳ · · · · · · · · ·

Q: What kind of beans don't grow in a _____?
(place)
A: Jelly beans.

· · · · · · · · ✳ · · · · · · · · ·

Did you hear about the dog that swallowed a **firefly**? He _____ with de**light**.
(verb)

· · · · · · · · ✳ · · · · · · · · ·

Q: What did the _____ say to the **ham**?
(noun)
A: Nice to **meat** you!

Q: What do you call a **fossil** that doesn't ever want to _____?
(verb)
A: Lazy **bones**!

* * * * * * * * * ✳ * * * * * * * * * * *

Q: How did the **lemon** get into the crowded _____?
(place)
A: It **squeezed** itself in.

* * * * * * * * * ✳ * * * * * * * * * * *

"Do you want to hear a _____ joke
(adjective)
about a **cat**?"

"Sure!"

"Just **kitten**, I don't have one."

Q: What is as big as a _____ but doesn't
(noun)
weigh anything?
A: Its **shadow**.

. . . . ✳ . . . .

Q: How did the _____ become a **pickle**?
(food)
A: It went through a **jar**ring experience.

. . . . ✳ . . . .

Q: What did the five fingers say to
the _____?
(noun)
A: Nothing. Fingers can't talk.

. . . . ✳ . . . .

Q: Why didn't the _____ win the race?
(fruit)
A: It ran out of **juice**.

DAD JOKE LEVEL:

☆EXPERT☆

(Now fill in the blanks to make the punchlines work!)

I knew a _____ in school who got
   (animal)
straight A's. He was a wise **quack**er.

. . . . ★ . . . .

Q: What kind of _____ do **drummers**
   (food)
love best?
A: Beets!

. . . . ★ . . . .

Q: Who **cleans** the _____?
   (place)
A: Mer**maids**.

. . . . ★ . . . .

Did you hear about the _____ who got
   (animal)
detention? She was **horsing** around.

Q: Why did **Tiger Woods** return

the _____?
(food)

A: Because there was a **hole in one**.

* * * * * * * ⭐ * * * * * * * *

You can't play _____ with **mountains**.
(game)

They're always **peak**ing.

* * * * * * * ⭐ * * * * * * * *

Q: What _____ is always **crying**?
(noun)

A: The **weeping** willow.

* * * * * * * ⭐ * * * * * * * *

Q: What do **Eskimos** eat when they vacation

in _____?
(place)

A: **Brrr**itos.

LOL

Q: What is the _____'s favorite TV
(noun)
show?
A: Whale of fortune.

* * * * * * * * * ⭐ * * * * * * * * *

When I _____ my **voice**, I was
(verb)
speechless.

* * * * * * * * * ⭐ * * * * * * * * *

Q: What kind of _____ are good friends?
(noun)
A: Rose buds.

* * * * * * * * * ⭐ * * * * * * * * *

That student never does his _____
(school subject)
homework on time. He's a **calcu-later**.

* * * * * * * * * ⭐ * * * * * * * * *

Q: Why did the **ice cream** become
a _____?
(profession)
A: It wanted to get the **scoop**.

Q: Where does the _____ go when it
(animal)
needs a haircut?

A: To the **baa-baa** shop.

. . . . ✳ . . . .

My **math book** looks really _____. I
(emotion)
think it has a lot of **problems**.

. . . . ✳ . . . .

Q: What do you call a _____ cow?
(adjective)

A: Beef **jerk**y.

. . . . ✳ . . . .

Q: How do you get two **peaches**
to _____?
(verb)

A: **Pit** them against one another.

. . . . ✳ . . . .

Guitars must be _____. They're
(adjective)
always getting **picked** on.

118

MY FIRST
DAD JOKES

(Write your own jokes below!)

_____

_____

_____

_____

_____

_____

_____

_____

_____

_____

_____

120

LOL